Write, DRAW, Believe

✝✝✝

75+ Faith-Building Activities for Christian Kids

To all truth seekers- May you find the one and only Truth!
-Alex B.

This journal is dedicated to every Christian obedient enough to follow God with their entire heart. May God give you the strength to follow His calling.
-Alyssa B.

Copyright © 2020 Alyssa Brulz and Alex Brulz
All rights reserved.
ISBN: 9798645304508

CREATE A ME PAGE

Write 3 fun facts about yourself, create a short biography, and paste a photo of yourself.

1. _____

2. _____

3. _____

— **GENESIS 1:27** —

Set a timer for 2 minutes and write down as many names for Jesus as you can think of before the timer goes off.

Prince of Peace

SAVIOR

The Shepherd

— ISAIAH 9:6 —

WRITE A "RECIPE" FOR *Salvation*

— ROMANS 10:9 —

- HEBREWS 13:5 -

- MATTHEW 6:19-20 -

Write "Jesus Loves Me" in all caps with something from nature.

- JEREMIAH 31:3 -

– Psalm 95:1 –

WRITE A SONG TO GOD.

- EPHESIANS 5:19 -

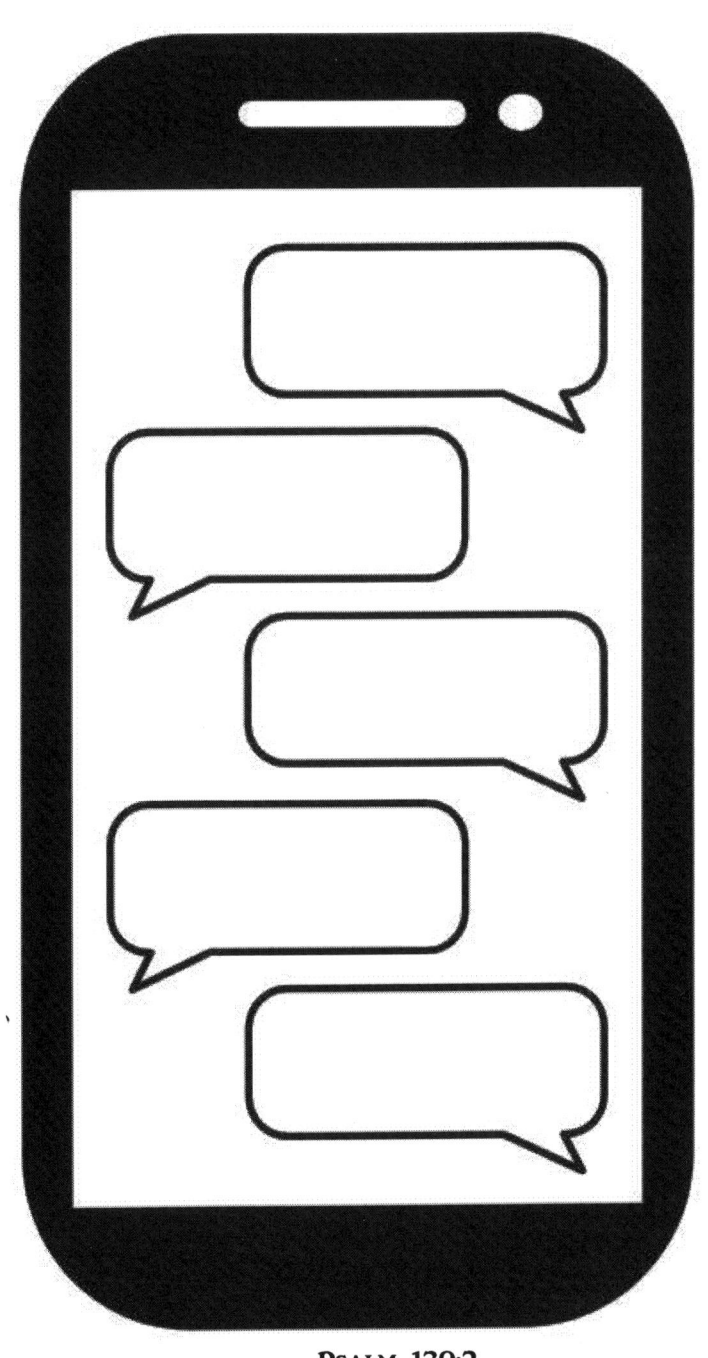

Imagine you are texting with Jesus. What would you say?

– Psalm 139:2 –

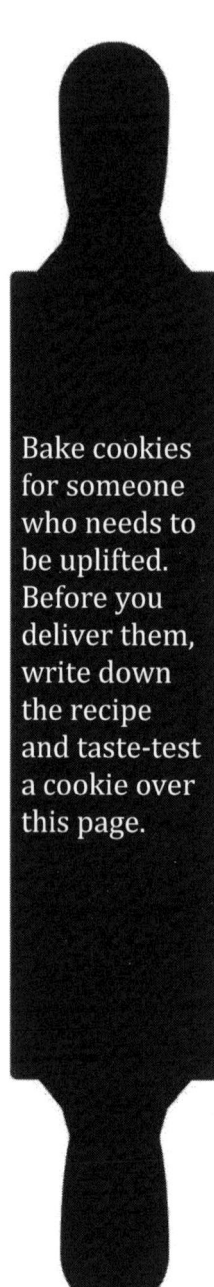

Bake cookies for someone who needs to be uplifted. Before you deliver them, write down the recipe and taste-test a cookie over this page.

– 1 Thessalonians 5:11 –

Wanted

Design a wanted poster for someone in the Bible. Don't forget the reward- we are precious to God!

- JOHN 3:16–17 -

JESUS

- Hebrews 13:8 -

- JOHN 1:1 -

- Psalm 119:11 -

Find sand and tape it to this page. God can count every grain in the entire world!

– Psalm 139:17-18 –

 Pretend you're a realtor selling part of heaven. Make a listing and describe what heaven looks like. It's the best place ever!

- JOHN 14:2 -

– PHILIPPIANS 3:20 –

Write a message to Jesus that you can read in a mirror.

– JAMES 1:22–25 –

WRITE WHAT YOUR NAME MEANS:

_____
_____
_____
_____
_____
_____
_____
_____

NOW WRITE WHAT YOU MEAN TO GOD:

_____
_____
_____
_____
_____
_____
_____
_____
_____
_____
_____

- PROVERBS 22:1 -

What makes a good leader? Write attributes of one inside this crown.

– HEBREWS 13:7 –

God loves His creation! Find a furry pet to play with and tape some of its fur here.

- PROVERBS 12:10 -

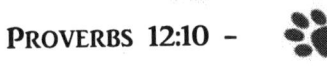

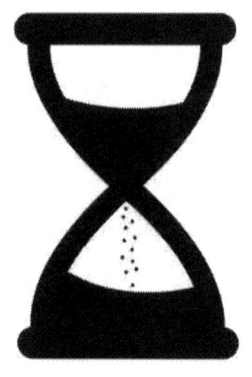 WRITE A LETTER TO YOUR FUTURE SELF. IN IT, TELL YOURSELF TO STAY STRONG IN THE FAITH AND NEVER WALK AWAY FROM GOD.

- 2 Corinthians 13:5 -

- Psalm 9:1 -

Put the Old Testament books in order on the lines.

Genesis
Exodus
Leviticus
Numbers
Deuteronomy
Joshua
Judges
Ruth
1 Samuel
2 Samuel
1 Kings
2 Kings
1 Chronicles
2 Chronicles
Ezra
Nehemiah

— COLOSSIANS 3:16 —

Put the New Testament books in order on the lines.

2 John
John
Jude
1 Corinthians
1 Peter
Revelation
Hebrews
Matthew
2 Corinthians
Titus
2 Thessalonians
Philemon
3 John

1 Thessalonians
Romans
Galatians
2 Peter
Acts
1 Timothy
Luke
James
Colossians
1 John
Ephesians
Mark
Philippians
2 Timothy

_____
_____
_____
_____
_____
_____
_____
_____
_____
_____
_____
_____
_____
_____
_____
_____
_____
_____
_____
_____
_____
_____
_____
_____
_____
_____
_____

- 2 Timothy 3:16 -

WRITE DOWN EVERYTHING YOU'RE AFRAID OF. WHEN YOU'RE DONE, TAKE CRAYONS AND SCRIBBLE OUT YOUR FEARS.

– 1 Peter 5:7 –

Write down everything you're *Thankful* for. Make sure to cover the whole page!

- 1 Chronicles 16:34 -

 Imagine you are a news reporter reporting on an event in the Bible. Explain everything that happened and write down what you would say on this page.

- COLOSSIANS 4:6 -

WRITE DOWN SOME SINS ON THIS PAGE. THEN, USE A PAIR OF SCISSORS TO CHOP IT INTO SHREDS.

When we are saved, our sins are forgiven and forgotten.

- 1 JOHN 1:9 -

DRAW

SOMETHING FROM CREATION. TRY TO BE AS DETAILED AS YOU CAN! EVEN STILL, GOD IS MORE DETAILED.

- ROMANS 1:20 -

Jesus shed His blood to pay the penalty for your sins. Turn this entire page red.

− 1 John 1:7 −

- Matthew 28:18-20 -

Fill this rainbow with different colors. Don't use the same material twice!

- Genesis 9:12-16 -

- REVELATION 10:1 -

- Isaiah 40:31 -

WRITE ABOUT WHEN YOU WERE SAVED.

Jesus is the light of the world. Draw a lightbulb and color it bright yellow.

- JOHN 8:12 -

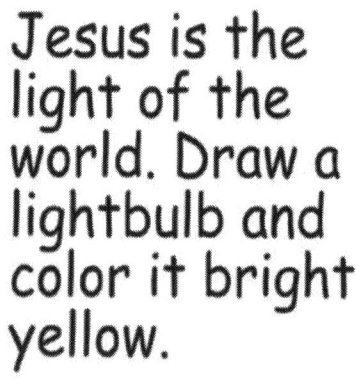

Write "Jesus" in different handwriting inside the cross.

- DEUTERONOMY 31:6 -

Paste a seed in the magnifying glass.

- Matthew 17:20 -

DESIGN A POSTER TELLING EVERYONE WHAT CHRISTMAS IS REALLY ABOUT.

- LUKE 2:1-21 -

Draw a comic strip of the creation timeline.

Before Creation	Day One

Day Two	Day Three

Day Four	Day Five

– GENESIS 1 –

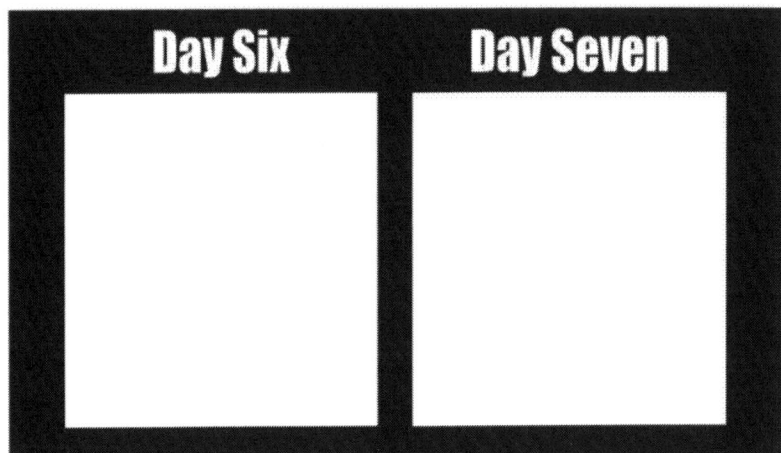

Day Six

Day Seven

After Creation

− Genesis 2 −

Write a prayer to God in colorful markers or pencils.

_____

_____

_____

_____

_____

_____

_____

_____

_____

_____

_____

_____

_____

_____

_____

– 1 THESSALONIANS 5:17–18 –

Make a list of ways you can
VOLUNTEER
and then try to do those things.

1. _____
2. _____
3. _____
4. _____
5. _____
6. _____
7. _____
8. _____
9. _____
10. _____
11. _____
12. _____
13. _____

- 1 Peter 4:10 -

CUT OUT MAGAZINE CLIPPINGS AND PASTE THEM TOGETHER TO MAKE A MADE-UP CREATURE. WRITE A DESCRIPTION TO GO ALONG WITH YOUR INTERESTING ANIMAL.

- HEBREWS 3:4 -

 Go outside and describe in one paragraph what you hear, see, taste, touch, and smell.

- PSALM 96:11-12 -

FIND BIBLE VERSES TO *REMEMBER* WHEN YOU'RE DOWN.

- PHILIPPIANS 4:6-7 -

– DEUTERONOMY 31:8 –

Draw the Armor of God on this page.

- EPHESIANS 6:10-18 -

Punch holes in the circles and string any color yarn through them. Be creative with your designs!

– Mark 8:34 –

 The fruit from the tree of knowledge of good and evil may not have been an apple. Write or draw what you think it might have looked like.

– GENESIS 2:16–17 –

WRITE A PRAYER TO GOD ASKING FOR FORGIVENESS

– Psalm 86:5 –

NOW WRITE A NOTE FORGIVING SOMEONE ELSE

– COLOSSIANS 3:13 –

Make your own version of Joseph's coat of many colors using tissue paper, wrapping paper, or fabric.

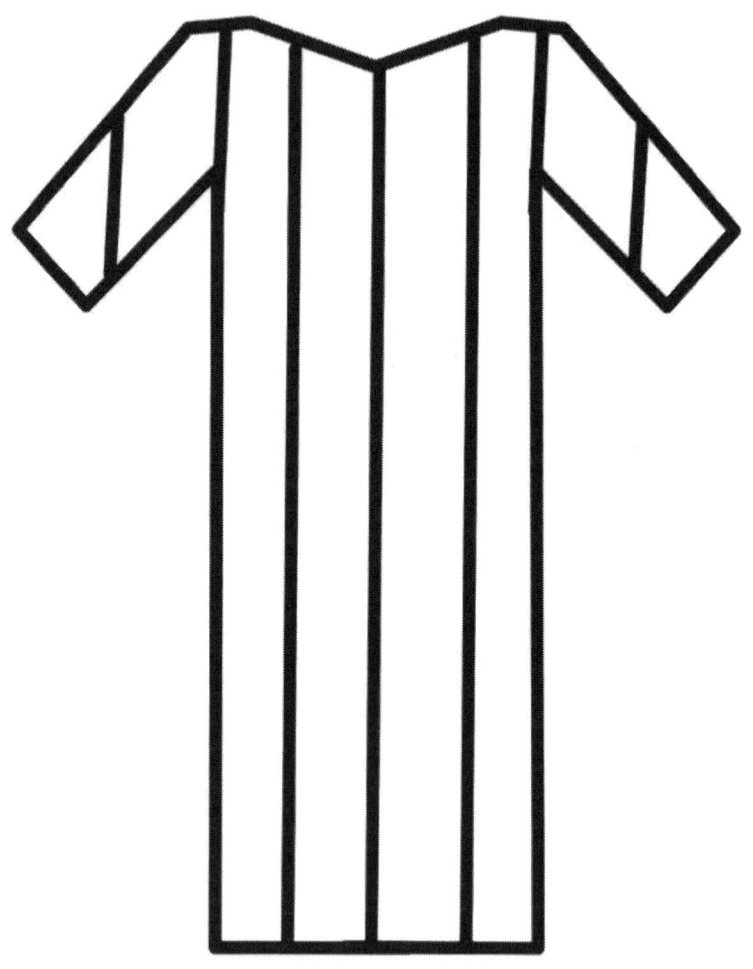

- GENESIS 37:3 -

Find a picture of your favorite animal and staple it here.

- MATTHEW 6:26 -

Write a prayer to God for someone you know who hasn't accepted Christ as his or her Savior.

— JEREMIAH 29:12 —

Fill out this multiple choice quiz.

1. If your neighbor asks if you are a Christian, do you...
   a. Deny it
   ↓b. Tell them "yes"
   c. Ignore them
   d. Other:_____

2. If someone asks you a question about your faith and you don't know the answer, do you...
   a. Avoid the topic
   b. Make up a random answer
   c. Say, "I'll get back to you on that" but never really do
   d. Work to find the real answer
   e. Other:_____

- 1 PETER 3:15 -

3. You just got $50. Your church is having a fundraiser. Do you...
    a. Say you don't have any money
    b. Save your money so there's more to donate later
    c. Donate all of your new money
    d. Donate part of your new money
    e. Other:_____

4. If there are kids in your Sunday School class being rude when the teacher is trying to talk, do you...
    a. Yell at them
    b. Ignore them
    c. Quietly tell them they are being disruptive and politely ask them to stop
    d. Other:_____

– 2 CORINTHIANS 9:7 –

- PSALM 119:105 -

Make a roadmap with signs that lead to Jesus.

– JOHN 14:6 –

- 1 TIMOTHY 4:12 -

 Make this page a bright color. Jesus is always the brightest!

– NUMBERS 6:25 –

Press flowers on these pages.

— LUKE 12:27 —

- Matthew 6:28-30 -

WRITE A SHORT STORY ABOUT A CHRISTIAN. IT HAS TO INCLUDE BIBLE VERSES AND THE WORDS UMBRELLA, BELIEVE, FRENCH FRIES, AND TOUGH.

_____
_____
_____
_____
_____
_____
_____
_____
_____
_____
_____
_____
_____
_____
_____
_____

- PSALM 96:3 -

- Mark 9:23 -

Write an uplifting message to a friend. Then, have them write one back to you.

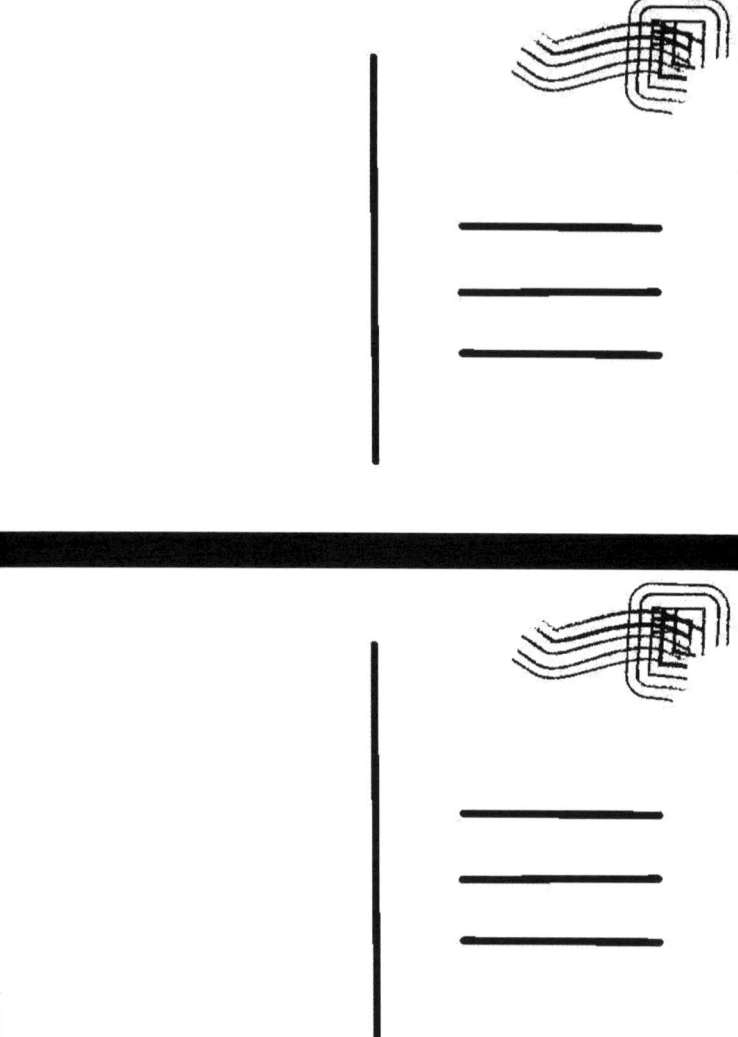

- 1 JOHN 4:7 -

Make a paper snowflake and place it on this page. God made each snowflake unique. He made you unique, too!

- JOB 37:6 -

 Pretend you are planning a vacation. Make a collage of things to do and write about the place. Heaven will be even better!

- Exodus 13:21 -

- MARK 6:32 -

- JEREMIAH 10:12 -

Start a collection on these pages to remind yourself of God's amazing power.

– 1 Chronicles 29:11 –

You are the salt of the world! Sprinkle salt on this page and leave it here.

- Matthew 5:13 -

Write a list of ways you have volunteered in the past.

— 1 Corinthians 10:31 —

LEARN HOW TO SAY "JESUS IS MY SAVIOR" IN AT LEAST FIVE DIFFERENT LANGUAGES. WRITE THE TRANSLATIONS DOWN IN DIFFERENT COLORS.

— Genesis 11:1–9 —

– 1 Corinthians 14:10 –

MAKE A MOSAIC SPELLING OUT "HE IS RISEN".

— 1 CORINTHIANS 15:3-4 —

Make sheep without using paint, crayons, markers, pencils, or pens.

- John 10:27 -

 *Jesus is the best gift ever! Cover this page with wrapping paper.*

– ROMANS 6:23 –

Write about the best gift you have ever recieved.

Jesus

- 2 Corinthians 9:15 -

Write a list of things you're good at and how you can use them for God's glory.

- JAMES 1:17 -

DRAW A PICTURE OF WHAT YOU THINK YOU'LL LOOK LIKE IN 10 YEARS. THEN, WRITE A SHORT PARAGRAPH ABOUT WHAT YOU THINK YOU'LL HAVE ACCOMPLISHED.

_____

_____

_____

_____

_____

_____

_____

_____

_____

- JEREMIAH 29:11 -

write a secret message that only you and God can decode.

– MATTHEW 6:6 –

Write a question about the Bible. Talk to trusted believers and reference the Scriptures to find an answer.

I don't know:_____

I found out:_____

_____

_____

_____

_____

_____

_____

So my answer is:_____

_____

_____

_____

_____

_____

_____

- PSALM 25:4 -

– Hebrews 10:25 –

Paste **SOUVENIRS** from church events here!

- ROMANS 15:5-6 -

God, thank you for...

1.

2.

3.

4.

5.

6.

7.

8.

9.

10.

– Colossians 3:15 –

11.

12.

13.

14.

15.

16.

17.

18.

19.

20.

21. AND SO MUCH MORE!

- 1 Chronicles 16:34 -

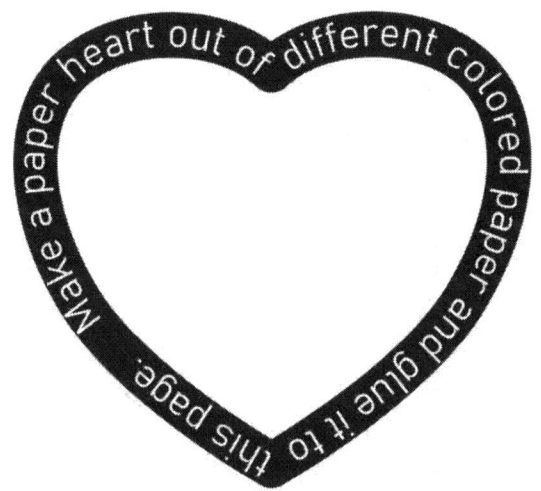

– 1 Corinthians 16:14 –

DO ANYTHING YOU WANT ON THESE PAGES!

– Ephesians 2:10 –

– 1 Corinthians 10:31 –

WRITE GOALS TO HELP STRENGTHEN YOUR FAITH.

- PROVERBS 19:21 -

- PSALM 20:4 -

COLLECT BUSINESS CARDS FROM VARIOUS NON-PROFITS AND CHRISTIAN PLACES.

- Mark 16:15 -

- ROMANS 8:28 -

**MAKE LEAF RUBBINGS ON THIS PAGE.
PASTE THE LEAVES YOU USED ON THE OPPOSITE PAGE.
IF YOU CAN, WRITE THE KIND OF PLANT EACH IS FROM.**

- Psalm 1:3 -

– REVELATION 22:2 –

Write about a time when God clearly provided for you.

– PHILIPPIANS 4:19 –

DRAW YOUR OWN PLANET.

– PSALM 19:1 –

Write, draw, or paste something in each of these circles that remind you of the fruit of the Spirit.

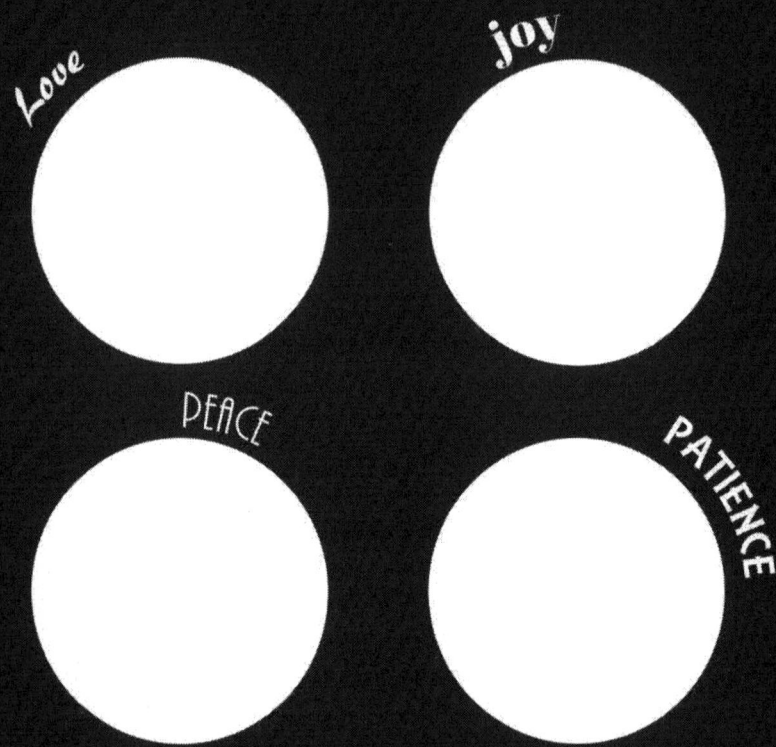

- GALATIANS 5:22-23 -

MAKE A COMMITMENT TO BE STRONG IN YOUR CHRISTIAN WALK.

I, _____, promise to always trust God and let Him be my guide. I believe He loves me and sent His Son to die in my place, so I can be safe from my sins and spend eternity with Him. I have asked Him to make me a new person and forgive my sins, and I trust He has done both. I plan to stay strong in my Christian walk and use everything I have to help further His kingdom. I want to follow God's will for my life, no matter where it takes me.

Signed: _____

Date: ___/___/___

– PROVERBS 16:3 –

WRITE "THIS IS NOT THE END" IN BOLD LETTERS.

— REVELATION 22:21 —

Alyssa Brulz is a Christian, twelve-year-old homeschooled student. She really likes to write and design graphics. She illustrated the picture book *Aah! Blown Away, Crash!: An Alphabet Misadventure.*

Alex Brulz is a Christian homeschooled student. She spends much of her time with her sister and best friend, Alyssa. Alex is an aspiring writer and blogger. She looks forward to seeing what God has in store for her life.

IMAGE CREDITS

Cover Image- JLG from Pixabay
Camera- Alyssa Brulz
Alarm Clock- Alyssa Brulz
Apron- George Mutambuka from Pixabay
Gift Tags- Alyssa Brulz
Feather- Mohamed Hassan from Pixabay
Viola- Chrom72 from Pixabay
Headphones- Gordon Johnson from Pixabay
Smart Phone- Alyssa Brulz
Rolling Pin- Alyssa Brulz
Arrow- Elias Schäfer from Pixabay
Bible- Alyssa Brulz
Sand Castle- Alyssa Brulz
House- Alyssa Brulz
For Sale Sign- Alyssa Brulz
Crown- Alyssa Brulz
Dog and Cat- Elisabeth Leunert from Pixabay
Paw prints- Elias Schafer from Pixabay
Hourglass- Alyssa Brulz
Fish One- Alyssa Brulz
Crayon- Alyssa Brulz
Rabbit- OpenClipart-Vectors from Pixabay
Microphone- Alyssa Brulz
Scissors- simisi1 from Pixabay
Tropical Leaf- rsull from Pixabay
Paper Airplane- Alyssa Brulz
Rainbow- Alyssa Brulz
Fish Two- Alyssa Brulz
Cross and Arrow- Alyssa Brulz
Lighthouse- Alyssa Brulz

IMAGE CREDITS

Cross- Alyssa Brulz
Magnifying Glass- Alyssa Brulz
Comic Strip- Alyssa Brulz
Gears- Alyssa Brulz
Swan- Mudassar Igbal from Pixabay
Pine Tree- Alyssa Brulz
Shield- Alyssa Brulz
String Cross- Alyssa Brulz
Apple- Alyssa Brulz
Horses- guilaine from Pixabay
Joseph's Coat of Many Colors- Alyssa Brulz
Notebook Paper- Alyssa Brulz
Road- Alyssa Brulz
Light Bulb- Alyssa Brulz
Bee- yabayee from Pixabay
Umbrella- Alyssa Brulz
Postcard- Alyssa Brulz
Snowman- Alyssa Brulz
World- gian andra from Pixabay
Binoculars- gian andra from Pixabay
Hammer- Alyssa Brulz
Salt Shaker- Alyssa Brulz
Grass- Canva
Present- Alyssa Brulz
Banner- Alyssa Brulz
Rock- Alyssa Brulz
Heart- Alyssa Brulz
Leaf- Alyssa Brulz
Hands- Alyssa Brulz

Manufactured by Amazon.ca
Bolton, ON